12F IN GIVING UP

DAF EDUCATION
Best in Australia

Engineer Manoj Mudiyanselage

Copyright © 2023 by Author Name.Manoj Mudiyanselage

All rights reserved. No part of this book may be used or reproduced in any form whatsoever without written permission except in the case of brief quotations in critical articles or reviews.

For more information, or to book an event, contact :
(Email : manojsura7@yahoo.com)

Book design by DAF Education in Australia
Cover design by DAF Education in Australia

First Edition : April 2023

About the Author

Registered Professional Engineer in Queensland and Chartered Professional Engineer, Manoj has 23 years of experience in a wide range of civil engineering disciplines. In addition to his technical expertise, he has extensive experience in managing complex and multidisciplinary projects in Singapore and Australia. Manoj is the project manager responsible for the planning to finalisation of the construction projects. Manoj was responsible for managing all ten elements of project management, including key stakeholders such as property owners, local MPs, City Councils, and the heavy vehicle industry.

Acknowledgments

I would like to express my sincere gratitude to my wife, Nadika, for her invaluable guidance, support, and encouragement throughout the entire process of writing this book. Her insights, comments, and suggestions were instrumental in shaping my ideas and improving the overall quality of the manuscript.

I am also deeply grateful to my colleagues, friends, and family members who provided me with their unwavering support, encouragement, and inspiration. Their feedback, suggestions, and words of encouragement were immensely helpful and greatly appreciated.

I would like to acknowledge the contributions of the project team members who provided invaluable assistance in collecting and analysing data. Their hard work and dedication were instrumental in the successful completion of this project.

Finally, I would like to thank the publisher for their support and assistance in bringing this book to fruition. Their professionalism, expertise, and commitment to quality were instrumental in ensuring that this book met the highest standards of excellence.

If ever I have worked with a courageous, resolute thinker who persists without regard for fear of failure or any other limiting F, it's Manoj. This book is very reflective of the author's professional ethic and approach to challenges in and outside of the workplace. A worthy read!

Dylan Hesselberg FIEAust FAIPM, Head of Property PMO - The Salvation Army

I have worked with the Author for many years at various locations and note that he has put in a lot of experience into words. He has stated that giving up is never an option but directing your energy towards a new goal is the best solution. This is very true and can take away the effects of failure from a person. This book is a good read to enhance our ability to tackle failure as the words come from real life experience.

Prasenjit Bhattacharyya, Civil Engineer, M.Eng, MIEAUST, RPEQ

This handy guide by Manoj will keep you positive, inspire you and remind you to never give up. We all face tricky times, even the best of us have failed, feared, and fallen. This book clearly shows the most recognised world leaders, public figures and musicians have clearly suffered, but they never gave up. This great book of facts will help you face your fears, get you to keep going and to never give up. I recommend this book to anyone who feels like giving up, experiencing challenges, and needs some inspiration! A handy book for your work desk or coffee table to refer to each day!

Jennifer Griffiths-Communications Advisor

I met Manoj at university time, and I got to know him as a very enthusiastic young individual who had eager to take every challenge in his life for a better future. Manoj never gave up any opportunity in his life, never had a fear of future. That character brought him to the place where he is in his life today. Manoj has written this simple meaningful book to reflect his life experiences. Read this book and learn one small thing to change your life tomorrow.

Nilakshi Fernando- University Colleague

This book depicts the author's personality, expertise, life experience, and maturity towards the diverse aspects of human reactions in coping with challenges in distinct life contexts. Let me CONGRATULATE him for producing this psychologically insightful piece of work by penetrating through the internal conflicts of the human mind. Further, he has been able to present an admirably succinct account of each chapter in such a way to entangle the reader with its fascinating yet profound content with utmost clarity. I am sure this book will invariably catch a large readership in no time and set them free of " mind-forg'd manacles".

DON'T GIVE UP!

Read this **CONFIDENCE BOOSTER** and feel the **SELF-TRANSFORMATION** at any moment of despair. Priyanka Kumarasinghe (Visiting faculty- English, SANASA Campus, Sri Lanka)

CONTENTS

12F IN GIVING UP I

ABOUT THE AUTHOR 1

ACKNOWLEDGMENTS 2

POPULAR PEOPLE FAILED 6

F1. FEAR OF THE FUTURE 10

F2. FEEL THE WORLD OWES THEM SOMETHING 13

F3. FEAR OF FAILURE MORE THAN DESIRE SUCCESS 16

F4. FEEL THEY HAVE SOMETHING TO LOSE 20

F5. FEEL SORRY FOR THEMSELVES 22

F6. FAILURE AS THE SIGNAL TO TURN BACK 26

F7. FEEL THEIR PROBLEMS ARE UNIQUE 31

F8. FOND OF OVERWORK 34

F9. FAIL TO BELIEVE IN THEMSELVES 37

F10. FAILING BY STUCK IN THE PAST 41

F11. FACING OVERWHELMING CHALLENGES 43

F12. FAIL TO RESIST CHANGE 46

NEURO-LINGUISTIC PROGRAMMING (NLP) TECHNIQUES ... 49

CHAPTER 1

Popular people failed

Giving up can be a complex and emotional decision. It can be tempting to give up when faced with difficult challenges or setbacks, but it is important to consider the potential consequences of doing so. In some cases, giving up may lead to missed opportunities or feelings of regret.

On the other hand, there are also situations were giving up may be the best option. For example, if a goal is no longer realistic or feasible, it may be more productive to redirect one's efforts towards a new goal.

Ultimately, the decision to give up or persist should be based on a careful consideration of one's goals, values, and circumstances. Seeking advice and support from trusted friends, family members, or professionals can also be helpful in making such decisions.

i. **Steve Jobs:** Steve Jobs is a legendary figure in the tech industry, but he was fired from his own company, Apple, in 1985. He later returned to Apple in 1997 and helped turn it into the powerhouse it is today.

ii. **Oprah Winfrey:** Before Oprah became the queen of talk shows, she was fired from her first job as a television reporter. She was told she was "unfit for TV."

iii. **Michael Jordan:** Michael Jordan is widely regarded as the greatest basketball player of all time, but he was cut from his high school basketball team as a sophomore.

iv. **J.K. Rowling:** J.K. Rowling's Harry Potter series is one of the most successful book franchises of all time, but she was rejected by 12 publishers before finally getting her first book published.

v. **Walt Disney:** Walt Disney is a household name, but he was fired from his first job as a newspaper editor because he "lacked imagination."

vi. **Beyonce:** Beyonce's girl group, Destiny's Child, was dropped by their first record label because they didn't think they had "star potential."

vii. **Albert Einstein:** Albert Einstein is one of the most brilliant minds in history, but he didn't speak until he was four and was considered a slow learner in school.

viii. **Vincent Van Gogh:** Vincent Van Gogh is one of the most famous artists in history, but during his lifetime he sold only one painting and was often mocked and criticized by his peers.

ix. **Thomas Edison:** Thomas Edison is credited with inventing the light bulb, but it took him over 1,000 attempts before he finally succeeded.

x. **Abraham Lincoln**: Abraham Lincoln is known as one of the greatest U.S. presidents, but he lost several elections before finally being elected president.

12F in giving up

xi. Stephen King: Stephen King is one of the most successful authors of all time, but his first novel was rejected 30 times before it was finally published.

xii. Elvis Presley: Before becoming the king of rock and roll, Elvis was told by the manager of the Grand Ole Opry that he should go back to driving a truck.

xiii. Richard Branson: Richard Branson, founder of Virgin Group, had many failed business ventures before achieving success with Virgin Records.

xiv. Mark Cuban: Billionaire entrepreneur and owner of the Dallas Mavericks, Mark Cuban, was fired from his first job as a computer salesman.

xv. Colonel Sanders: Colonel Sanders, the founder of Kentucky Fried Chicken, was rejected by over 1,000 restaurants before finding success with his secret recipe.

xvi. Jim Carrey: Before becoming one of the most successful actors of his time, Jim Carrey was booed off stage during his first stand-up comedy performance.

xvii. Madonna: Madonna was fired from her first job at Dunkin' Donuts for squirting jelly filling all over a customer.

xviii. Albert Schweitzer: Albert Schweitzer, a philosopher, physician, and musician, failed his first university entrance exam.

xix. Henry Ford: Henry Ford, founder of the Ford Motor Company, had two failed automobile companies before finding success with the Model T.

xx. Steven Spielberg: Steven Spielberg was rejected from film school three times before eventually attending and later becoming one of the most successful film directors in history.

xxi. Madonna: Madonna's first acting job was in the film "A Certain Sacrifice," which went straight to video.

xxii. Eminem: Eminem failed the 9th grade three times and dropped out of high school at the age of 17.

xxiii. **Jennifer Aniston:** Jennifer Aniston, famous for her role in the television show "Friends," was fired from her first television show, "Molloy.

CHAPTER 2

F1. Fear of the future

People give up because of **fear of the future** because they are often worried about what might happen and the uncertainties that come with it. Fear of the future can manifest in various ways, such as **anxiety** about the unknown, worry about making the wrong decision, or concerns about not being able to handle challenges that may arise.

In some cases, people may have had negative experiences in the past, which have made them more fearful of what might happen in the future. They may also lack confidence in their ability to handle difficult situations and feel overwhelmed by the thought of uncertainty and change.

"Giving up smoking is the easiest thing in the world. I know because I've done it thousands of times."
— **Mark Twain**

It's important to remember that fear is a natural emotion, and it's okay to feel afraid of the future. However, giving up is not the solution. Instead, it's essential to focus on building resilience, developing coping skills, and seeking support from loved ones or a mental health professional. By doing so, individuals can learn to manage their fears and face the future with greater confidence and optimism.

People may give up due to fear of the future for several reasons. Here are a few possible explanations:

1. **Uncertainty:** The future is often unknown, and this uncertainty can be scary. People may worry about what could happen and how they would cope if things didn't go as planned.
2. **Lack of Control:** People may feel like they have no control over what happens in the future, which can be frightening. This lack of control can make people feel powerless and overwhelmed.
3. **Negative past experiences:** If people have had negative experiences in the past, they may worry that the same thing will happen again in the future. This can make them hesitant to take risks or pursue new opportunities.
4. **Anxiety and Depression:** Anxiety and depression can make people feel hopeless and unable to imagine a positive future. They may believe that things will never get better, leading to a sense of hopelessness and despair.

It's important to note that fear of the future is a common feeling and can be addressed with the help of a therapist, support from loved ones, and self-care practices. By taking small steps towards building a positive future, people can overcome their fears and create a better tomorrow.

One example of a famous person who experienced failure due to fear of the future is Vincent van Gogh, the renowned Dutch painter. Van Gogh's story is marked by a series of personal and professional challenges that eventually led to his tragic end.

During his lifetime, van Gogh struggled with mental health issues and emotional instability. He battled with bouts of depression, anxiety, and ultimately was diagnosed with bipolar disorder. This constant internal turmoil often made it difficult for him to find stability and contentment.

In the late 1880s, Van Gogh's art career began to show promise. He started to receive recognition for his unique style and expressive use of color. However, the artist's fear of the future and uncertainty about his artistic success haunted him. He worried that he wouldn't be able to sustain his career or financial stability, and this fear overshadowed his artistic achievements.

Van Gogh's anxiety about his future worsened when his relationship with his brother Theo, who supported him both emotionally and financially, deteriorated. The strain on their relationship, combined with van Gogh's increasing mental health issues, led to a period of intense distress and self-doubt.

In the face of his fears, van Gogh's work began to suffer. He experienced creative blocks and struggled to produce paintings at the same pace as before. He became consumed by self-criticism and doubt, often considering his own artistic efforts as failures.

The culmination of van Gogh's fears and emotional turmoil occurred in 1890 when he tragically took his own life at the age of 37. His death came at a time when his artistic genius was not fully recognized, and his work only gained widespread acclaim after his passing.

Van Gogh's story serves as a poignant reminder of how the fear of the future and self-doubt can hinder even the most talented individuals. It highlights the importance of mental well-being, support systems, and finding ways to overcome personal fears to fulfill one's potential. Despite his tragic end, van Gogh's artistic contributions continue to inspire and resonate with people around the world today.

CHAPTER 3

F2. Feel the world owes them something

People may *feel that the world owes them something* for a variety of reasons, such as societal conditioning, entitlement, or a sense of victimhood. However, this mindset can lead to feelings of frustration, disappointment, and a lack of motivation. When people believe that they are entitled to certain things, they may become complacent and fail to take responsibility for their own lives.

In addition, when people feel that the world owes them something, they may develop unrealistic expectations that are not grounded. This can lead to a sense of entitlement that is difficult to satisfy and can make it hard for people to appreciate what they already have.

"When things go wrong, don't go with them."
— Elvis Presley

Furthermore, this mindset can prevent people from acting and making positive changes in their lives. When individuals feel that they are owed something, they may not feel motivated to work hard or strive for their goals, as they may believe that they are entitled to success without putting in the necessary effort.

Ultimately, it is important for individuals to recognize that they are responsible for their own lives and outcomes, and that success and happiness are the result of hard work, perseverance, and taking responsibility for one's own actions.

People may feel that the world owes them something due to a variety of reasons, such as a sense of entitlement, past experiences of privilege or success, societal messages that reinforce the idea of personal exceptionalism, and more.

However, when individuals believe that the world owes them something, they may become disappointed and disillusioned when they face challenges or setbacks. This can lead to feelings of frustration, anger, and helplessness, and may ultimately cause them to give up on their goals or aspirations.

"Give up trying to make me give up"
— __Masashi Kishimoto__

It's important to recognize that the world does not owe anyone anything, and that success is often the result of hard work, perseverance, and a willingness to learn from failure. By adopting a growth mindset and taking responsibility for their own actions and outcomes, individuals can overcome obstacles and achieve their desired outcomes.

One true story of a famous person who believed that the world owed them something is that of Kanye West, a renowned American rapper, producer, and fashion designer. Kanye West has publicly expressed his belief that he is owed recognition and opportunities due to his artistic talent and contributions to the entertainment industry.

Throughout his career, Kanye West has made numerous controversial statements and engaged in attention-grabbing behaviour, often expressing his frustration with the perceived lack of acknowledgment and respect he receives. In various interviews and public appearances, he has asserted that he is one of the greatest artists of all time and should be given more prominent positions in the music and fashion industries.

One notable incident occurred during the 2009 MTV Video Music Awards when Kanye West famously interrupted Taylor Swift's acceptance speech for Best Female Video, expressing his belief that Beyoncé deserved the award instead. This incident sparked widespread criticism and showcased his sense of entitlement, with many perceiving his actions as an attempt to overshadow and belittle others to uplift himself.

Moreover, Kanye West has frequently voiced his grievances about not receiving the level of support and recognition he believes he deserves from the fashion industry. He has openly expressed frustration with not being embraced as a high-end fashion designer and has called for more opportunities and respect in that field.

It's important to note that while Kanye West has displayed a sense of entitlement and a belief that the world owes him something, he has also faced personal struggles and challenges throughout his life, including battles with mental health issues. This context helps to provide a more nuanced understanding of his behaviour and mindset.

Ultimately, Kanye West's story serves as a reminder that even famous individuals can struggle with feelings of entitlement and the belief that they are owed something by the world, despite achieving significant success in their respective fields.

CHAPTER 4

F3. Fear of failure more than desire success

There are several reasons why people may give up due to the ***fear of failure more than the desire for success***. Here are a few possible explanations:

1. Negative bias: Humans are wired to pay more attention to negative experiences and thoughts than positive ones. This is known as negativity bias. Therefore, the fear of failure may feel more intense and compelling than the desire for success.
2. Self-doubt: Many people struggle with self-doubt and lack of confidence, which can make the fear of failure feel even more overwhelming. They may feel that they are not good enough or capable enough to succeed, leading them to give up before even trying.
3. Perfectionism: Perfectionism is a trait characterized by a strong desire to achieve flawless results and avoid mistakes at all costs. This mindset can lead people to become paralysed by the fear of failure, as they believe that any mistake or imperfection is unacceptable.
4. Social pressure: Society often places a lot of emphasis on success

and achievement, leading people to feel pressure to perform and succeed. This pressure can make the fear of failure feel more intense, as it is seen as a sign of inadequacy or weakness.

Overall, the fear of failure is a common experience for many people, and it can be a powerful barrier to achieving success. However, by recognizing and understanding the underlying reasons for this fear, individuals can begin to develop strategies to overcome it and pursue their goals with greater confidence and resilience.

"There is no failure except in no longer trying."
— Elbert Hubbard

People may give up due to fear of failure more than desire for success because failure is often seen as a negative outcome, while success is viewed as a positive outcome. As humans, we are wired to avoid negative outcomes as a means of self-preservation, and this includes avoiding failure.

Additionally, failure can often be associated with feelings of shame, embarrassment, and disappointment, which can be difficult to deal with. Fear of these negative emotions can cause people to avoid taking risks and trying new things, which are necessary for achieving success.

On the other hand, the desire for success may not be strong enough to overcome the fear of failure for some people. They may not fully believe in their ability to achieve success or may not have a clear vision of what success looks like for them. This lack of clarity and belief can lead to a lack of motivation and effort towards achieving success.

Ultimately, both fear of failure and desire for success are important factors in shaping our behaviour and decisions. It's important to recognize and address our fears and limitations, while also staying motivated and focused on our goals.

One true story of a famous person who had a fear of failure greater than the desire for success is that of Michael Jordan, widely regarded as one of the greatest basketball players of all time. Despite his immense talent and accomplishments, Jordan's fear of failure played a significant role in his career and drove him to push himself to unprecedented heights.

Throughout his career, Michael Jordan faced numerous challenges and setbacks. In high school, he was initially cut from the varsity basketball team, which fuelled his determination to prove himself. He used this failure as motivation, working tirelessly to improve his skills and eventually earning a spot on the team.

During his professional career with the Chicago Bulls, Jordan faced intense pressure to win championships and live up to the expectations placed upon him. His fear of failure became a driving force behind his relentless work ethic and dedication to the game. Jordan famously said, "I've missed more than 9,000 shots in my career. I've lost almost 300 games. Twenty-six times I've been trusted to take the game-winning shot and missed. I've failed over and over and over again in my life. And that is why I succeed."

Jordan's fear of failure motivated him to constantly strive for improvement, both physically and mentally. He was known for his rigorous training routines, his competitiveness, and his relentless pursuit of perfection. He used setbacks and losses as opportunities for growth and learning, fuelling his desire to bounce back stronger.

His fear of failure was evident in crucial moments during games, where he often stepped up and made game-winning plays. Jordan's competitiveness and refusal to let fear hold him back propelled him to achieve six NBA championships and earn five MVP awards, solidifying his status as an icon in the basketball world.

Michael Jordan's story serves as a reminder that fear of failure can be a powerful motivator. Rather than allowing it to paralyse him, he channelled his fear into determination and used it as a catalyst for success. His relentless pursuit of excellence and unwavering dedication continue to inspire athletes and individuals across various fields.

12F in giving up
CHAPTER 5

F4. Feel they have something to lose

People may give up on something when they **feel they have something to lose** because they fear the potential negative consequences of continuing to pursue that goal. This fear can stem from a variety of sources, such as the possibility of failure, disappointment, or rejection.

For example, imagine someone who is considering applying for a new job that they are interested in. However, they feel that if they apply for the job and don't get it, they will lose their current job or damage their reputation at work. This fear of losing their current job or reputation may cause them to give up on the idea of applying for the new job altogether.

"When we can't dream any longer we die."
— **Emma Goldman**

Similarly, people may give up on relationships, hobbies, or other pursuits if they fear that they will lose something important to them by continuing to pursue them. However, it's important to remember that giving up too easily can also lead to missed opportunities and regret. It's important to weigh the potential risks and rewards of a situation before deciding, and to not let fear hold us back from pursuing our goals and dreams.

The fear of losing something they value, such as a job, a relationship, or a reputation, can be so overwhelming that they may choose to avoid taking risks or pursuing their goals altogether.

Additionally, people may feel a sense of attachment or emotional investment in the things they stand to lose, making it difficult for them to let go and move on. They may also tend to focus on what they stand to lose rather than what they stand to gain, which can lead to a sense of paralysis and indecision.

"It's always to soon to quit!"
— **Norman Vincent Peale**

Ultimately, whether someone chooses to give up in the face of potential loss is a complex decision that depends on their personal values, motivations, and mindset. Some people may be more willing to take risks and accept the possibility of failure, while others may be more risk-averse and cautious.

CHAPTER 6

F5. Feel sorry for themselves

People may give up when they feel sorry for themselves because this mindset can lead to a sense of victimhood and powerlessness. When individuals focus on their own suffering and difficulties, they may become trapped in a cycle of self-pity and negativity, which can make it difficult for them to act and make positive changes in their lives.

Furthermore, feeling sorry for oneself can lead to a lack of personal responsibility. When individuals see themselves as victims of circumstance, they may be less likely to take ownership of their choices and actions and may be more likely to blame external factors for their problems. This can make it harder for them to identify and address the root causes of their challenges and may prevent them from developing the skills and resilience needed to overcome them.

"I would have stayed a hundred times and I would have left one time only - still, I left."
— Mihail Drumeş

It's important for individuals to acknowledge and validate their feelings of sadness and disappointment, but also to recognize that they have agency and control over their lives. By shifting their focus from their own suffering to acting and finding solutions, individuals can develop a sense of empowerment and motivation, which can help them overcome their challenges and achieve their goals.

People may give up when they feel sorry for themselves because self-pity can be a powerful demotivator. When individuals focus on their own negative emotions and circumstances, they may become overwhelmed by feelings of hopelessness and despair, which can make it difficult for them to act or make progress toward their goals.

"A real scientist solves problems, not wails that they are unsolvable."
— **Anne McCaffrey, Acorna: The Unicorn Girl**

Self-pity can also lead to a sense of victimhood, where individuals feel that their problems are the result of external circumstances beyond their control. This can make it harder for them to take responsibility for their situation and to identify concrete steps they can take to improve their lives.

To overcome self-pity and regain motivation, it can be helpful to focus on the things that are within one's control and to take proactive steps to improve one's situation. This might involve seeking support from friends or loved ones, setting small achievable goals, or taking concrete steps to address the challenges one is facing. By shifting the focus away from negative emotions and toward actionable steps, individuals can regain a sense of agency and motivation, and move forward with a renewed sense of purpose.

One true story of a famous person who felt they had something to lose is that of Elon Musk, the entrepreneur and CEO of companies such as Tesla and SpaceX. Throughout his career, Musk has consistently

12F in giving up

demonstrated a deep sense of responsibility and a fear of losing the progress he has made in various ground-breaking ventures.

Elon Musk's story is characterized by his relentless pursuit of ambitious goals in industries such as electric vehicles, renewable energy, and space exploration. With Tesla, he aimed to revolutionize the automotive industry by making electric vehicles mainstream. Similarly, with SpaceX, he sought to reduce the cost of space travel and eventually colonize Mars. These ventures were not only driven by a desire for success but also by a profound belief in the urgent need for sustainable solutions and the importance of expanding humanity's presence beyond Earth.

Musk's sense of having something to lose is evident in his relentless work ethic and attention to detail. He has been known to work long hours and involve himself deeply in the day-to-day operations of his companies. His commitment to these ventures goes beyond financial gains, as he recognizes the potential positive impact they can have on the world.

Furthermore, Musk has publicly acknowledged the risks involved in his ventures. He has stated that he feels a strong responsibility toward his shareholders, employees, and customers, knowing that their trust and investments are at stake. He has frequently expressed concern about potential setbacks and the possibility of failure, highlighting the high stakes and the importance of mitigating risks.

Musk's drive to succeed and his fear of losing what he has built have been instrumental in his ability to rally teams and overcome significant challenges. While he has faced numerous obstacles and setbacks along the way, his relentless pursuit of his goals and his willingness to take calculated risks have propelled him to achieve remarkable milestones.

Elon Musk's story exemplifies the mindset of someone who

recognizes the significance of their endeavours and the potential losses associated with them. His fear of losing ground serves as a motivating factor, pushing him to continue innovating and striving for success in his ventures.

12F in giving up
CHAPTER 7

F6. Failure as the signal to turn back

People may give up when they see ***failure as a signal to turn back*** because they may view failure as a reflection of their personal inadequacies or limitations. When individuals experience setbacks or failures, they may feel discouraged and lose confidence in their ability to succeed. This can lead them to believe that their efforts are pointless or that they are not capable of achieving their goals, causing them to give up or turn back.

Additionally, some individuals may have a fixed mindset that views failure as a permanent and unchangeable state. They may believe that their abilities and intelligence are predetermined and that they cannot improve or grow beyond their current level. This can lead to a lack of motivation and a sense of helplessness in the face of challenges, causing them to give up when they encounter setbacks.

"No one gives up on something until it turns on them, whether or not that thing is real or unreal."
— Thomas Ligotti, Teatro Grottesco

However, it's important to remember that failure is a natural part of the learning process and can provide valuable feedback and opportunities for growth. By reframing failure as a chance to learn and improve, individuals can develop a growth mindset that enables them to persevere through challenges and achieve their goals. With persistence, determination, and a willingness to learn from setbacks, individuals can overcome failure and achieve success.

"A real scientist solves problems, not wails that they are unsolvable."
— **Anne McCaffrey, Acorna: The Unicorn Girl**

It's important to remember that failure is a natural part of the learning process and can provide valuable feedback and insights into how to improve and move forward. By reframing failure as a necessary step on the path to success, individuals can learn to approach challenges with resilience and perseverance, rather than giving up at the first sign of difficulty. This can help them build confidence, develop new skills, and achieve their goals in the long term.

One true story of a famous person who saw failure as a signal to turn back is that of J.K. Rowling, the acclaimed author of the Harry Potter series. Before her immense success, Rowling faced numerous rejections and setbacks in her writing career. However, instead of giving up, she used failure as a motivation to persevere and pursue her dreams.

Rowling's journey to becoming a published author was marked by hardship and rejection. She experienced personal struggles, including the death of her mother and a failed marriage, while living as a single mother on welfare. Despite these challenges, she remained determined to write and tell her stories.

When she first completed the manuscript for Harry Potter and the Philosopher's Stone, Rowling faced rejection from multiple publishers. Twelve publishing houses turned down her book before Bloomsbury, a small publishing company, took a chance on her manuscript. Even after securing a publisher, Rowling encountered initial from some literary agents who did not believe the book would succeed.

Rowling's story could have ended with those rejections, but she viewed failure as a signal to continue rather than turn back. She used these setbacks as fuel to refine her work and seek out opportunities elsewhere. Her unwavering belief in her story and her refusal to give up ultimately led to the immense success of the Harry Potter series, which has sold millions of copies worldwide and spawned a highly successful film franchise.

Throughout her career, Rowling has openly discussed the role failure played in her journey. She has emphasized that failure is an inevitable part of the creative process and a steppingstone towards success. Rowling's resilience and determination to push through failure have made her an inspiration to aspiring writers and individuals facing their own challenges.

Rowling's story serves as a reminder that setbacks and failures should not be seen as reasons to abandon one's dreams. Instead, they can be valuable learning experiences that provide the opportunity for growth and improvement. By viewing failure as a signal to persist rather than retreat, Rowling demonstrated the power of resilience and the transformative potential of perseverance.

One true story of a famous person who saw failure as a signal to turn back is that of Thomas Edison, the renowned American inventor and businessman. Edison's relentless pursuit of innovation was fuelled by his unwavering determination and refusal to give up, even in the face of repeated failures.

Edison is best known for his work on the electric light bulb, but his journey to success was far from smooth. It took him thousands of attempts and numerous failures before he finally discovered the right materials and design for a practical and commercially viable light bulb. Edison famously said, "I have not failed. I've just found 10,000 ways that won't work."

Throughout his career, Edison encountered setbacks and obstacles that could have discouraged him from pursuing his inventions. However, he saw failure not as a reason to quit but as an opportunity to learn and refine his ideas. Each unsuccessful attempt provided him with valuable information that brought him closer to achieving his goals.

In addition to his work on the light bulb, Edison faced challenges in other areas of his inventions. For instance, his efforts to create a practical storage battery were met with repeated failures and setbacks. Yet, he persisted, believing that each failure brought him one step closer to success. Eventually, he achieved significant breakthroughs in battery technology, which had a lasting impact on various industries.

Edison's ability to embrace failure as a learning experience and a steppingstone to success is a testament to his resilience and perseverance. His approach allowed him to see setbacks not as definitive defeats but as opportunities to gather knowledge, adjust, and continue forward.

Edison's story serves as a powerful reminder that failure is not the end but rather a part of the journey towards success. It highlights the importance of persistence, adaptability, and a mindset that views failure as a valuable feedback mechanism rather than a reason to give up.

12F in giving up

Through his determination and willingness to learn from his mistakes, Thomas Edison became one of history's most prolific inventors, leaving a lasting impact on the world.

CHAPTER 8

F7. Feel their problems are unique

People *fell that their problems are unique* because they may feel that their situation is so different from others that no one else can relate or understand. This can lead to feelings of isolation, loneliness, and helplessness, which can cause them to give up.

However, the truth is that while everyone's problems may have unique aspects, there are often commonalities between them. For example, many people struggle with issues related to relationships, finances, or health. By assuming that their problems are unique, people may miss out on the support and advice that others can offer, which can make a big difference in finding solutions and coping strategies.

"No one gives up on something until it turns on them, whether or not that thing is real or unreal."
— Thomas Ligotti, Teatro Grottesco

It's important to remember that seeking help and sharing one's struggles with others can be a sign of strength, not weakness. By opening to trusted friends, family members, or professionals, people can gain new perspectives, ideas, and strategies for dealing with their challenges.

12F in giving up

People may give up when they assume their problems are unique because they may feel isolated and helpless. When individuals believe that they are the only ones facing a particular challenge, they may feel like they have no one to turn to for support or guidance. This can lead to feelings of hopelessness and despair, which can make it difficult for them to persevere in the face of adversity.

Additionally, assuming that one's problems are unique can also create a sense of shame or embarrassment. If individuals believe that their struggles are unusual or abnormal, they may be reluctant to seek help or share their experiences with others. This can lead to a cycle of isolation and avoidance that can make it even harder to overcome their difficulties.

"Resignation is what kills people. Once they've rejected resignation, humans gain the privilege of making humanity their footpath."
— Kouta Hirano

It's important to remember that while everyone's experiences are unique to some extent, many people face similar challenges and can offer valuable support and advice. By reaching out to others and seeking help when needed, individuals can gain the perspective and resources they need to tackle their problems and achieve their goals.

One true story of a famous person who felt that their problems were unique is that of Marilyn Monroe, the iconic American actress and model. Throughout her life, Monroe struggled with various personal and emotional challenges, leading her to believe that her problems were distinct from those faced by others.

Marilyn Monroe's rise to fame was accompanied by a range of

personal difficulties, including a tumultuous childhood, a history of mental health issues, and struggles with substance abuse. Despite her success as a Hollywood star, she often felt isolated and misunderstood, believing that her experiences were uniquely her own.

Monroe's fame brought her immense public scrutiny, with media attention focused not only on her talent but also on her personal life and relationships. This intensified her sense of uniqueness and the belief that her problems were singularly complex. Monroe struggled with insecurities, seeking validation and love while dealing with the pressures of maintaining her image and public persona.

While many people face challenges similar to those experienced by Monroe, her perspective on her problems stemmed from a combination of her personal struggles, public persona, and the societal expectations placed upon her as a sex symbol and Hollywood icon.

Monroe's belief in the uniqueness of her problems was evident in her introspective nature, as reflected in her diaries and writings. She often expressed a longing for connection and understanding, searching for a deeper meaning in her experiences and relationships.

Tragically, Monroe's life was cut short when she died at the age of 36. Her struggles with mental health, substance abuse, and the pressure of fame contributed to her untimely death, leaving behind a legacy of a talented but deeply troubled woman who felt her problems were uniquely her own.

Marilyn Monroe's story serves as a reminder that even those who appear glamorous and successful can grapple with personal challenges and a sense of isolation. It highlights the importance of empathy and understanding towards individuals who may believe that their problems are unique, emphasizing the need for support and compassion in navigating the complexities of life.

CHAPTER 9

F8. Fond of overwork

There are several reasons why people ***fond of overwork.*** Here are some possible explanations:

1. **Burnout**: Overwork can lead to burnout, which is a state of physical, emotional, and mental exhaustion. Burnout can make people feel like they have nothing left to give, and they may give up on their work as a result.

2. **Stress:** Overwork can be stressful, and too much stress can lead to anxiety and depression. When people feel overwhelmed by their workload, they may give up because they don't know how to manage their stress.

3. **Lack of support:** If people feel like they're working too much without enough support, they may feel like giving up. Lack of support can take many forms, including not enough time off, no help with tasks, or a lack of recognition for hard work.

4. **Health problems:** Overwork can lead to health problems, such as exhaustion, insomnia, and chronic illness. When people's health suffers because of their workload, they may give up because they can't physically or mentally handle the demands of their job.

5. **Lack of motivation:** When people feel like their work doesn't matter or they're not making progress, they may lose motivation and give up. This can happen when people are working too much and not seeing the results

they want.

"Im dying everyday
My breakfast are cigarettes and coffee
My lunch is depression
My snacks are regrets
My dinner are memories and anger
My night is non stoping tears
Sleep is my death
Waking up the next day and here we go again dying everyday"
— Ali hassan hasan

One true story of a famous person who was fond of overwork is that of Steve Jobs, the co-founder of Apple Inc. Known for his relentless drive and passion for his work, Jobs was notorious for his long hours and dedication to pushing the boundaries of innovation.

Throughout his career, Jobs was deeply involved in every aspect of Apple's products and operations. He was known for his meticulous attention to detail and his insistence on perfection, often working late into the night and on weekends to ensure that every element of Apple's products met his high standards.

Jobs' commitment to his work extended beyond regular office hours. He would frequently bring work home, immersing himself in the creative process and exploring new ideas. His passion for innovation was unparalleled, and he expected the same level of dedication from his employees.

One famous anecdote that showcases Jobs' fondness for overwork is the development of the original iPhone. During its development, Jobs demanded an impossible deadline, insisting that the teamwork around the clock to deliver a ground-breaking product. His uncompromising work ethic and drive to push boundaries led to the successful launch of the iPhone, which revolutionized the mobile phone industry.

However, Jobs' overwork tendencies had a toll on his personal life and health. His relentless pursuit of perfection and dedication to his work often led to strained relationships and burnout. In 2004, he was diagnosed with pancreatic cancer, a disease that ultimately took his life in 2011.

While Jobs' fondness for overwork is well-documented, it is essential to note that overworking is not a sustainable or healthy approach to success. While his work ethic and dedication played a significant role in Apple's success, it is important to balance work with personal well-being and relationships.

Steve Jobs' story serves as a cautionary tale, reminding us of the potential consequences of excessive work and the importance of maintaining a healthy work-life balance. It is crucial to find a balance between ambition and self-care, acknowledging that true success encompasses not only professional achievements but also personal fulfillment and overall well-being.

CHAPTER 10

F9. Fail to believe in themselves

People may give up and ***fail to believe in themselves*** for various reasons. Some common reasons include:

1. **Past failures:** If someone has experienced repeated failures in their life, they may begin to lose confidence in their abilities and start to doubt themselves.

2. **Negative self-talk:** As mentioned earlier, negative self-talk can be a significant barrier to self-belief. If someone constantly tells themselves that they are not good enough or capable enough, they may start to believe it.

3. **Fear of failure:** Fear of failure can be a powerful force that can cause people to give up on their dreams and stop believing in themselves. They may worry about what others will think or believe they are not good enough to succeed.

4. **Lack of support:** If someone does not have a supportive network of family, friends, or colleagues, it can be challenging to maintain a positive mindset and believe in oneself.

5. Comparison to others: Comparing oneself to others can be detrimental to self-belief. When someone constantly measures their success against others, it can be challenging to maintain a healthy sense of self-worth and belief in one's abilities.

12F in giving up

It's important to note that giving up and losing self-belief is a common experience that many people face at some point in their lives. However, with the right mindset, support, and effort, it is possible to overcome these obstacles and regain a strong sense of self-belief.

"It's hard to give up the being together with someone."
— **Lois Lowry, <u>A Summer to Die</u>**

It is important for individuals to believe in themselves, as self-belief is crucial for personal growth, development, and success. However, sometimes people may struggle with self-doubt and lose their self-belief. If you find yourself in this situation, there are a few things you can do to regain your self-belief:

1. **Identify and challenge negative self-talk:** Negative self-talk can be a significant barrier to self-belief. It is essential to recognize these negative thoughts and challenge them with positive affirmations.

2. **Set realistic goals:** Setting achievable goals and working towards them can help boost your confidence and reinforce your belief in yourself.

3. **Celebrate your successes**: Celebrate even the smallest of accomplishments, as this can help build confidence and reinforce self-belief.

4. **Surround yourself with positivity**: Surround yourself with people who support and encourage you and avoid negative influences that may bring you down.

5. **Practice self-care:** Taking care of yourself both physically and mentally is crucial for self-belief. Make sure to take time for yourself, exercise, eat healthily, and get enough rest.

Remember that self-belief is not something that comes naturally to everyone and can take time and effort to develop. However, with perseverance and the right mindset, anyone can develop a strong sense of self-belief.

"He has no talent at all, that boy! You, who are his friend, tell him, please, to give up painting.

—-Manet to Monet, on Renoir---"

One true story of a famous person who struggled with self-belief and experienced failures is that of Walt Disney, the visionary behind the Disney entertainment empire. Throughout his career, Disney faced numerous rejections and setbacks that tested his belief in himself and his creative ideas.

In the early years of his career, Walt Disney faced several failures and disappointments. He started his first animation company, Laugh-O-Gram Studio, in Kansas City, but it eventually went bankrupt. Undeterred by this setback, Disney moved to Hollywood and founded the Disney Brothers Studio with his brother Roy. However, they struggled to find success, and their first character, Oswald the Lucky Rabbit, was taken away from them by their distributor.

One of Disney's most iconic creations, Mickey Mouse, initially faced rejection as well. The original concept for Mickey Mouse, then known as Mortimer Mouse, was turned down by distributors who claimed it would not appeal to audiences. However, Disney persisted and reworked the character into the lovable Mickey Mouse we know today. Mickey Mouse went on to become a global phenomenon, propelling Disney's success and cementing his legacy in the entertainment industry.

Disney's self-doubt was not limited to his early career struggles. When he embarked on creating the first full-length animated feature film, Snow White and the Seven Dwarfs, many people doubted its potential for success. The film was dubbed "Disney's Folly" by skeptics in the industry, who believed audiences would not sit through a feature-length cartoon. However, Disney believed in the project and went ahead with its production. Snow White and the Seven Dwarfs became a critical and commercial triumph, marking a significant milestone in the world of animation.

Throughout his life, Disney faced failures, financial challenges, and creative hurdles. However, he never let these setbacks diminish his belief in his own vision and ideas. His determination, resilience, and unwavering self-belief allowed him to overcome adversity and create a legacy in the entertainment industry.

Walt Disney's story is a testament to the power of self-belief and perseverance. Despite facing numerous failures and doubts, he persisted in pursuing his creative dreams and left an indelible mark on the world of entertainment. Disney's journey serves as an inspiration to those who may doubt themselves, reminding us that failures are not the end but opportunities for growth and eventual success.

CHAPTER 11

F10. Failing by stuck in the past

People may give up and get stuck in the past for various reasons. Some common reasons include:

1. **Trauma**: Traumatic experiences in the past, such as abuse, loss, or significant life changes, can leave a lasting impact on an individual's mental health and cause them to get stuck in the past.

2. **Regret:** Regret for past mistakes or missed opportunities can cause someone to dwell on the past and miss out on new experiences and opportunities.

3. **Nostalgia**: Nostalgia for a past time or place can make it difficult for someone to move on and focus on the present.

4. **Fear of the unknown**: Fear of the unknown future can make it tempting to cling to the past, where things are familiar and comfortable.

5. **Lack of closure:** When someone has not fully processed or come to terms with a past event or relationship, they may struggle to move on and get stuck in the past.

It's important to note that getting stuck in the past can have a negative impact on an individual's mental health and overall well-being. It's essential to take steps to process and move on from past experiences and focus on the present and future. Some strategies that can be helpful

12F in giving up

include seeking professional support, practicing mindfulness and self-reflection, setting goals, and focusing on personal growth, and cultivating a supportive network of friends and family.

"What's so good about giving up? Is it better to escape from reality to the point where you're throwing away your hope?"

— Hajime Isayama, Attack on Titan #1

CHAPTER 12

F11. Facing Overwhelming challenges

People are *facing overwhelming challenges* and feeling like you're failing. It can be incredibly tough to deal with difficult circumstances, but it's important to remember that everyone faces setbacks at some point in their lives. Here are a few suggestions for navigating through overwhelming challenges:

Break it down: Break your challenges into smaller, more manageable tasks or goals. This can make them feel less daunting and help you approach them step by step.

Seek support: Reach out to friends, family, or a support network for assistance and encouragement. Sometimes, discussing your challenges with others can offer new perspectives and potential solutions.

Prioritize self-care: Take care of yourself physically, emotionally, and mentally. Make sure you're getting enough rest, eating well, and engaging in activities that bring you joy and relaxation. Taking care of yourself will provide you with the strength to face challenges more effectively.

Learn from setbacks: Rather than viewing failures as definitive, consider them as learning opportunities. Reflect on what went wrong, identify areas for improvement, and use those insights to develop new strategies.

Seek guidance: If you feel overwhelmed and unsure how to proceed, don't hesitate to seek guidance from a mentor, coach, or professional who can provide expertise in the specific area you're struggling with.

Focus on what you can control: Concentrate on the aspects of your challenges that you have control over and work on those. Accept that some circumstances may be beyond your control and shift your energy toward making the best choices within your sphere of influence.

Celebrate small victories: Recognize and celebrate even the smallest wins along the way. Each step forward, no matter how small, is progress worth acknowledging.

Remember, it's okay to ask for help and take breaks when needed. Facing overwhelming challenges can be tough, but with time, perseverance, and the right mindset, you can find a way forward.

"Obstacles are those frightful things you see when you take your eyes off your goal." – Henry Ford

One true story of a famous person is the life of Oprah Winfrey. Oprah Winfrey is a renowned media mogul, talk show host, actress, and philanthropist. She is known for her influential talk show, "The Oprah Winfrey Show," which ran for 25 years and became one of the highest-rated television programs of its kind.

Oprah faced numerous challenges throughout her life. Born into poverty in rural Mississippi, she experienced a difficult childhood marked by poverty, abuse, and hardship. Despite these obstacles, Oprah persevered and found solace in her passion for communication and storytelling.

At the age of 19, Oprah began working in radio and eventually moved into television, where she gained recognition and popularity as a local news anchor. In 1986, she launched her own talk show, "The Oprah Winfrey Show," which went on to become a global phenomenon. The show tackled a wide range of topics, including personal development, self-help, and interviews with influential figures. Through her authenticity, empathy, and ability to connect with her audience, Oprah inspired millions of viewers worldwide.

Oprah's success expanded beyond her talk show. She ventured into acting, producing films, and founded her own media company, Harpo Productions. She has also used her platform to advocate for important social issues and has been a prominent supporter of education, literacy, and empowerment initiatives.

Despite her achievements, Oprah has remained humble and open about her struggles. She has openly discussed her experiences with childhood trauma, weight fluctuations, and personal growth. Through her transparency, she has inspired others to embrace their own journeys and overcome obstacles.

Oprah Winfrey's story is a testament to the power of resilience, determination, and the ability to transform one's life despite overwhelming challenges. She serves as an inspiration to many, demonstrating that with hard work, perseverance, and a commitment to personal growth, it is possible to overcome adversity and achieve remarkable success.

12F in giving up
CHAPTER 13

F12. Fail to resist change

There are many reasons why people *fail resist change* and eventually give up. Here are some common ones:

1. **Fear of the unknown**: People often prefer the familiar over the unknown, even if the familiar isn't working well for them. Change requires stepping into the unknown, which can be scary and uncomfortable.
2. **Loss of control:** Change can make people feel like they are losing control over their lives or their work. This can be unsettling and cause people to resist the change.
3. **Uncertainty about outcomes:** People may resist change because they are unsure of the outcomes that will result from it. They may worry that the change will make things worse rather than better.
4. **Comfort with the status quo:** People may resist change because they are comfortable with the way things are currently. Even if they recognize that change is necessary, they may prefer to stick with what they know.
5. **Lack of motivation:** Change can be challenging and require

effort. If people are not motivated to make the change, they may give up rather than persisting.
6. **Lack of support:** If people do not have support from others in making the change, they may feel overwhelmed and give up.

Overall, giving up on change can be a complex issue with multiple factors involved. It's important to understand the reasons behind resistance to change and work to address them to increase the chances of successful change.

"Giving up on the person you truly love is not the same as forgetting a nightmare."
— Pradip Bendkule

One true story of a famous person who struggled to resist change is Kodak. Kodak was a renowned photography company that dominated the industry for many years. However, as the world transitioned from film to digital photography, Kodak faced significant challenges in adapting to the changing market.

In the 1970s, Kodak invented the first digital camera. However, fearing that digital photography would cannibalize their profitable film business, Kodak failed to embrace the technology and capitalize on their own invention. They remained heavily invested in traditional film products and underestimated the speed at which digital photography would revolutionize the industry.

As digital cameras became more popular and smartphones with built-in cameras emerged, Kodak's market share declined rapidly. The company struggled to keep up with the changing consumer preferences and the convenience of digital photography. Despite attempts to transition into digital products later, Kodak's efforts fell short, and they eventually filed for bankruptcy in 2012.

The story of Kodak serves as a cautionary tale about the importance of adapting to change in the face of disruptive technologies. Despite their initial innovation in digital photography, Kodak's failure to embrace the shift and resistance to change ultimately led to their downfall. It highlights the significance of recognizing industry trends, consumer demands, and adapting business strategies accordingly to stay relevant in a rapidly evolving world.

CHAPTER 14

Neuro-Linguistic Programming (NLP) techniques

If you're looking for information on using Neuro-Linguistic Programming (NLP) techniques to help with giving up or quitting something, such as a habit or addiction, I can provide some guidance.

Set a clear goal: Clearly define what you want to give up and why. Make sure your goal is specific, measurable, achievable, relevant, and time-bound (SMART).

Understand your motivation: Explore the reasons behind your desire to give up. Identify the benefits and drawbacks of your current behavior and the advantages of quitting.

Anchoring positive states: NLP techniques often involve anchoring positive states of mind. Identify a positive state or feeling that will support your efforts to quit. Visualize yourself successfully giving up and experience the positive emotions associated with it. Then create an anchor, such as squeezing your thumb and forefinger together, to recall that positive state whenever needed.

Reframing: Reframing is a technique used in NLP to change how you perceive a situation. Identify any limiting beliefs or negative thoughts associated with quitting and reframe them into positive and empowering beliefs. For example, instead of thinking, "I'll never be able to quit," reframe it as, "I have the ability to overcome challenges and make positive changes in my life."

Visualization: Visualization is a powerful technique used in NLP. Close your eyes and imagine yourself successfully giving up the habit. Visualize the process, the challenges you may face, and how you will overcome them. See yourself living a healthier, happier life without the habit.

Anchoring negative states: NLP techniques also involve anchoring negative states to deter you from engaging in the habit you want to give up. Identify the negative consequences or feelings associated with your current behavior and create an anchor to recall those negative states whenever tempted to engage in the habit.

Pattern interruption: NLP suggests interrupting the patterns associated with the habit you want to give up. Identify triggers or situations that lead to engaging in the habit and find ways to interrupt those patterns. For example, if you tend to smoke after a meal, find an alternative activity or habit to replace it.

Seek support: NLP techniques can be used on your own, but having support from others can enhance your success. Consider joining a support group, finding an accountability partner, or working with a therapist trained in NLP or addiction recovery.

Remember that NLP techniques can be helpful, but they are not a substitute for professional help when dealing with serious addictions or mental health issues.

www.ingramcontent.com/pod-product-compliance
Lightning Source LLC
Chambersburg PA
CBHW040328220526
45473CB00009B/2606